Stacey Backpacks The World

FUN EXPLORATION AND ADVENTURE STORIES

George

Love & Hugs

from

Stacey Suter

STACEY SUTER

Balboa Press books may be ordered through booksellers or by contacting:

Balboa Press
A Division of Hay House
1663 Liberty Drive
Bloomington, IN 47403
www.balboapress.co.uk
UK TFN: 0800 0148647 (Toll Free inside the UK)
UK Local: 02036 956325 (+44 20 3695 6325 from outside the UK)

ISBN: 978-1-9822-8422-0 (sc)
ISBN: 978-1-9822-8423-7 (e)

Print information available on the last page.

Balboa Press rev. date: 09/24/2021

BALBOA.PRESS
A DIVISION OF HAY HOUSE

Dedication

I would like to dedicate this book to all those who dare to explore this planet we call home. There is so much to see and experience. Look up, and take it all in. Follow your curiosity, never stop dreaming, and as Dory always says, 'Just keep swimming.' Life really is a journey, so enjoy it.

Acknowledgements

I would like to thank my cousin Becky for inspiring me to see the world and being my role model, and my family for having all faith in me that I'd find my way to the correct terminal. I would also love to thank all the families who gave me a place to sleep, fed me, and stayed in touch with me all these years later. Thank you to Gerald, George, Emily, and Callum for proofreading my stories and helping me. Last but not least, merci beaucoup to Ophe, my talented illustrator for her heart-warming work.

Inspired by the tales of her cousin Becky's travels, Stacey was encouraged to seek out the same places so she could see them with her own eyes. After selling all her belongings, including her phone and car, and saving every penny she had earned at work for an entire year, Stacey bought flight tickets to explore eight countries around the world. Her backpack was full of all the things she would need, including a water bottle, a journal and pen, a camera, her passport, her flight tickets, a first aid kit, and lots of clothes! The first part of Stacey's journey was from her home in south Wales to Gatwick Airport in England with her family. Her family had bets on whether Stacey would actually go through with this adventure or even if she would just get lost in the airport. She said her goodbyes and waved to her family as she walked towards the terminal. The adventure of a lifetime was about to begin.

Stacey had to travel over five thousand miles on an aeroplane to get to the first country. Twelve hours later, she arrived in Thailand and walked out of the airport. The heat of the air hit her right in the face like when she opened a hot oven. On her first few nights away from home, she slept at a lovely little guest house called Baan Eve in a little village called Ayutthaya. It was owned by Sunchi and his two enormous Great Dane dogs, Baht and Yelhi. There were handmade wooden tables and benches in the dining area, the reception desk was made from a wooden boat, and there were lots of English books on display in the dining area because Sunchi's daughter was learning to speak English. Stacey, very tired from her long journey, found the perfect spot to sit and write in her journal about her trip so far while the dogs lay in the sun.

That evening, Stacey went in search of a nice local meal and saw her first temple, Wat Wihan Luang, which means 'the Grand Hall.' The sign outside explained, 'The Grand Hall is sixty-three metres long and twenty metres wide, with three staircases in the front.' All of the temples Stacey saw were enormous, with lots of detail in their stone walls, and were just magnificent to look at.

In the morning, Stacey excitedly hopped in a small taxi, which looked like it was half car and half motorbike, called a tuk-tuk, for a tour around nine different temples. It only cost her eight hundred baht (about eighteen British pounds). The temples were huge and had so many pretty details on them. They were amazing.

THAILAND

That afternoon, while walking through a street market and feeling all hot and sweaty, Stacey treated herself to a Thai iced tea, but instead of in a cup, it came in a plastic bag with a straw! To this day, this is Stacey's favourite drink, although she does prefer to use a cup.

A few days later, Stacey took an eleven-hour overnight train to Chaing Mai and went on a jungle trek with a tour guide called Joshua. After walking for miles through the jungle with a group of people, Stacey needed the toilet, but there were no toilets in the jungle so she left the group to find a quiet hiding place. While looking around to make sure no one could see her, Stacey noticed she had disturbed a nest of spiders! To her horror, millions of spiders came running out towards her. She ran away screaming back to her group as fast as she could. She told everyone what happened, and they all found it funny and laughed with Stacey.

The group soon arrived at a jungle village to rest, where they ate fried pumpkin for their dinner and slept overnight in huts made from bamboo. On the last day of the trip, everyone went on a bamboo raft ride down a river.

Stacey thought it would be a nice, slow, and relaxing ride, but soon she found out that the people sitting on the riverbank would splash her and her raft mates if they didn't look wet enough. Soon enough Stacey was soaked from head to toe. Her raft crashed into other rafts. A boy called Sebastian tried ducking as his raft passed a tree, but it hit him and he fell into the river. It was the funniest thing ever.

Just before she left Thailand, Stacey got to visit another temple called Wat Rong Khun, which was known as the White Temple. It was covered in thousands of tiny pieces of glass that shimmered in the sunshine. It was the prettiest temple she had ever seen and one she would never forget.

The trip to the second country was not Stacey's favourite at all. It was a slow boat ride down the Mekong River to reach a place called Luang Probang in Laos. It took seventeen hours, and Stacey sat on a hard, wooden bench. Lots of people were crammed onto the boat. There were even people sitting on the floor. It was that full.

Even though it was the most uncomfortable boat trip ever, it was one of the most important trips Stacey had ever been on as she got to see some of the poorest parts of the world. She saw the children who lived in those parts of the world—saw them smiling and waving. They were so happy. Stacey learned that we don't need possessions like phones, the Internet, or televisions to have a reason to smile and be happy.

A few days later, Stacey set off with a tour guide named Pomme to visit a place called Plain of Jars in Phonsavan.

To get there, they had to travel on a road with eight thousand bends that twisted and climbed through the mountains. Stacey was not looking forward to the road trip because she knew that there were so many bends, but it was worth it.

The jars were bigger than Stacey had ever imagined. She couldn't even wrap her arms around them! They looked like humongous plant pots, and there were hundreds of them. Some were over three metres tall. Pomme asked, 'What do you think the jars were made for?' It was fun to hear everyone's ideas. Stacey thought they were made for people to hide in.

For the next adventure, Stacey travelled down to Vang Vieng to go cave tubing in a cave called Phu Kham.

She sat on a rubber dingy, strapped a head torch to her head, and followed her two tour guides, named Onn and Keo, into the cave. She pulled herself five hundred metres along a rope into the darkness. It was very scary, but then Stacey spotted hundreds of silkworms dangling from the ceiling glowing in the light of her head torch. It was amazing. She followed Onn and Keo out of the cave and down the river to find people along the riverbanks celebrating a water festival for the Laos New Year in April. Everyone splashed water at each other using buckets and water guns. It was a fun experience, but once again Stacey was soaked through. It was a good job Stacey had a waterproof bag to protect her camera! After a bit of encouragement, Stacey was brave enough to have a go on the river swing.

It was so high she almost didn't do it, but she leapt off the edge screaming, holding the swing handles so tightly. She didn't want to let go. After swinging back and forth, she finally let go and dropped into the water.

After all the New Year celebrations were over and Stacey was dry for the first time since being in Asia, she decided to write a postcard to her family and friends back home to let them know how much fun she was having while getting ready to move on to the next country.

Within the first hour of arriving in the third country, Vietnam, Stacey started searching for tickets to visit Ha Long Bay and Monkey Island with a New Zealand couple she became friends with named Kylie and Kyle.

When Stacey was out and about, a dear old lady asked if she would like to buy some pineapple. Stacey was delighted to, so she bought a small bag. The lady then insisted Stacey try on her hat and hold her fruit baskets for a photo. The dear lady took a quick photo of Stacey, popped her hat back on, threw her fruit baskets over her shoulder, and ran off down the street as fast as she could. To Stacey's horror, the dear old lady had charged Stacey 250,000 dong, which works out at nearly eight British pounds. Stacey was not impressed when she realised that she had been overcharged for the small bag of pineapple; the old lady was not so sweet after all. But Stacey was so pleased with the photo of her wearing the lady's hat, and the pineapple was so delicious, so she forgave the lady and carried on with her day.

The following morning, Stacey awoke early to get ready for her journey to the harbour, where she would board a ship that would take her and a group of other explorers to Ha Long Bay.

When the ship stopped, Stacey headed straight to the top deck to admire the scenery. The boat was surrounded by emerald-green waters, floating villages, and hundreds of tall islands made from limestone that looked like mini mountains. It took Stacey's breath away; it was out of this world.

Not wanting to leave Ha Long Bay, Stacey soon sat on another boat with Kylie and Kyle making their way to Monkey Island. When they arrived at the island, they dropped their bags inside their beach huts and then set off on an adventure to a beach where they discovered hundreds of monkeys playing hide-and-seek with one another. The monkeys were curious as to what food they could pinch from them. It was so much fun watching them. Stacey and the New Zealand couple could have stayed for hours watching them playing but decided to let the monkeys carry on with their fun in their natural habitat. They were so happy.

Stacey had been determined to try scuba diving just like her cousin Becky and got the opportunity in Vietnam.

She studied hard and trained every day out in the open waters. Stacey passed all her exams, and on her final skills test underwater, her instructor used his hand to signal OK. Then he gave Stacey a handshake, and in that moment, she knew she had qualified as a PADI-licensed scuba diver. Woohoo!

Following her curiosity of sea creatures, Stacey had so much fun exploring the seabed and the vibrant colours of the coral reefs. She even saw her favourite orange clown fish.

On to the fourth country, Cambodia. Stacey and Kylie hopped on a tuk-tuk the minute they arrived and explored the various sites of Phnom Penh. They saw lots of people sitting around and enjoyed watching the hundreds of monkeys lounging about in the heat or having a little wander; they seemed so happy and relaxed. This made Stacey's heart smile.

Stacey slept overnight at a hostel and then travelled on a bus to Siem Reap.

The following morning, she had to wake up at four thirty to meet her tuk-tuk driver, Vantha, for a tour of the temples of Angkor Wat.

CAMBODIA

Stacey thought she was clever by getting up early to beat the tourist crowds, but she was wrong. There were lots of people walking about. She decided to walk fast to get past all the crowds and found a quiet spot to take some photos of the sunrise hitting the temples.

The temples were enormous, and the engravings covering the walls were full of detail and character. It was mesmerising. Stacey was curious as to how they engraved such fine detail into the walls.

Her eyes lit up when she saw the temple called Ta Prohm. Massive tree trunks covered the entire roof, and the roots were tangled all around the entrance doors. They even covered the window areas and had grown over the floor surrounding the temple.

Whilst walking around the temples, Stacey saw a lot of children asking tourists to buy gifts or souvenirs from them.

Because Stacey loved the giant stone faces at the Bayon Temple, she made sure that when the tour was over, she went to a local gift shop where she purchased a wooden ornament to take home. Stacey still has this ornament sitting proudly on her windowsill.

When Stacey arrived back to her hostel room, she was really looking forward to feeling the cold air from the air conditioning to cool her down, but the hostel staff had turned it off so her room was boiling. Drenched in sweat, Stacey went to ask the staff to turn it back on as it was unbearable, but they refused. Stacey was not prepared to stay, so she packed her bags, checked out of the hostel, and hopped on a bus to leave the country immediately.

Her next stop was the fifth country, Australia. When Stacey's aeroplane landed, she went in search of a camper van to rent. She found one. It was bright green and very expensive. Stacey would spend the next three weeks driving from Cairns down to Sydney, approximately 1,500 miles.

AUSTRALIA

Out on the road, surrounded by beautiful mountains, the sun shining, driving past palm trees, parking up at various camp sites, sitting on white, sandy beaches while watching the surfers and dolphins swimming alongside each other was exactly what Stacey had imagined it would be.

Whilst driving, Stacey had her eyes on the lookout for kangaroos. Suddenly, she came across hundreds of them out in the wild. It was amazing!

AUSTRALIA

The day that Stacey had been dreaming about since she was a little girl finally came: she got to visit the zoo of Steve Irwin, the man from *The Crocodile Hunter* on TV. It was a seven-hundred-acre conservation and wildlife hospital owned by the Irwin family. Stacey got to meet a koala, feed the kangaroos, and visit the Crocoseum.

There was word that Steve's daughter, Bindi Irwin, was at the zoo that day, so Stacey became rather excited. Sadly, Stacey didn't get to see her but was over the moon that she got to meet a koala bear. She had a huge smile on her face all day.

Three weeks later, Stacey reached Sydney, where she spotted the Opera House, an iconic landmark. She shrieked with excitement the moment she saw it. It was such a huge and magnificent building. She parked the car and walked up closer to take some photos and finally explore Sydney.

FIJI

Soon Stacey arrived at the sixth country, Malolo Lailai, an island near Fiji. It was the most memorable greeting Stacey had ever experienced. The boat pulled up to the jetty and along came a group of Fijian men and women playing their guitars, clapping their hands, and singing songs. They placed a necklace made up of tiny seashells around Stacey's neck as a welcome gift.

Everyone was so friendly and said, 'Bula,' every time they walked past each other, which means 'hello.'

Stacey checked into her beach front room and headed straight out to snorkel, exploring the sea life and pretty colours of the coral reef. Snorkelling was so much fun. There were a lot of zebra fish, eels, and a tiny yellow fish that kept following Stacey.

In the evening after eating delicious Fijian food, Stacey enjoyed watching the Fijian dancers wearing grass skirts and flowers in their hair, and then the Mauri fire dancers came out. It was a wonderful night.

The next day, Stacey decided to go out on a kayak. After passing a few corners, Stacey began to feel a little tired, but it was too late to turn back so she kept paddling. She then became thirsty and hungry, and her arms hurt so much from paddling that she began to cry. She didn't think she was ever going to make it back to her resort, but it was worth it as the water was so crystal clear that she could see the sand at the bottom. There were fish jumping out of the water, and the scenery was beautiful.

Hours later, Stacey was glad to arrive back at the resort. A lady waiting to take Stacey's kayak out of the sea noticed that she was exhausted and upset so she insisted on helping her out of the water. The lady asked how far Stacey had gone, and when Stacey explained she had kayaked around the entire island, the lady was in shock and explained, 'The Island is roughly five hundred acres. That's a lot of miles.'

After resting all night, Stacey paid to go on a boat trip to visit a reef. On the boat, someone spotted a pod of dolphins jumping out of the water and having fun. Then someone thought they spotted a shark fin. The small group of people on the boat all looked with curiosity. The boat pulled up closer, and they soon realised the humongous body under the water was a whale shark: the largest fish in the sea. It must have been almost ten metres long.

The lads who were on the boat jumped into the water with their snorkels on to see the whale shark's spotty skin up close. Stacey's eyes opened wide in shock that they were so brave to get in the water with this ginormous creature.

Later that day, when back on the main island of Fiji, Stacey went scuba diving at a reef called the Edge. It was like a swimming next to a cliff edge. A huge turtle swam nearby, and then a white-tip reef shark appeared.

Stacey grabbed tightly onto her instructor's arm and didn't let go. To Stacey's relief, the shark was quite happy swimming around and minding its own business. It didn't seem bothered by the humans watching its every move.

After swiftly swimming away from the shark, it was time to ascend and hop back onto the boat and go to land.

Hiring the camper van in Australia had used up almost all of Stacey's savings. She had a difficult decision to make: accept defeat and go home early or find herself a job so her travels could continue. Stacey couldn't give up her dream. She had come this far and knew she may never get to go on this adventure ever again. Her flight tickets were already paid for, so it was on to the seventh destination, New Zealand, to hopefully find some work and top up her savings.

Stacey got to meet a lot of families and farmers. She found a website that specialised in helping backpackers find families who needed help on their farms in exchange for free meals and a place to sleep. Stacey made her way around some of the most amazing areas of both the north and south islands, working on different farms. Stacey's most memorable jobs were feeding the sheep on Angela's farm in Waipukarau, picking lemons from Fiona and Jerry's trees in New Plymouth, where their children Nadia and Ethan taught Stacey how to make the most amazing lemon cordial—yum—and working at the Store on the beach front in Kekerengu, owned at the time by the McFarlanes. They generously allowed Stacey to stay at their cottage where she met, worked, and lived with an amazing group of friends: Karen, Ed, Chessie, Esther, Michael, Craig and Ian. Stacey liked it here so much she stayed for seven months.

On Stacey's last day working at the Store, the others played a prank. They put Stacey's home-made brownies in the display cabinet and she sold them to customers all day, not knowing they were hers until they showed her the sign that said, 'Stacey's Brownies.'

Then there was the community house called Gricklegrass, where Stacey bottle-fed Ruby the lamb and was shown how to milk the cows by Ryan and Doree.

One morning in the early hours at Gricklegrass, Stacey was woken by a loud noise and the ground shaking. It was an earthquake. Stacey was afraid and didn't know what to do so she took shelter under a door frame.

The floorboards were swaying, and ornaments fell and smashed on the floor. It was terrifying.

The aftershocks lasted for days, so everyone had to keep themselves busy. When checking on all the animals outside, they witnessed the devastation the damage caused. All the way down the street, the lamp posts were leaning over, and there were huge cracks in the roads. She heard on the news the earthquake had a magnitude of 7.1, which was very high, and its epicentre was not far from where Stacey was living. No wonder it was so bad. It was so upsetting, but everyone was safe, which was all that mattered. Everyone got together and played board games at the dinner table with candles and head torches as the power lines had been cut.

A few weeks later, it was Stacey's birthday, and to celebrate, she drove over three hundred miles to Franz Josef Glacier.

NEW ZEALAND

She headed to the guided tours office, where she was handed a big pile of clothes to put on for safety and to keep warm. Everyone on the tour was given snow boots, waterproof trousers, a huge jacket, hat, gloves, and a bag that had spikes for the snow boots. The glacier was gigantic, and the ice was crystal clear with a hint of blue, like a huge diamond.

Stacey popped the spikes onto her boots and took her first steps on the glacier. It was an unbelievable feeling.

When they reached the top, everyone had to walk through a tunnel where Stacey asked, 'Do we really have to walk through there?' She remembered her cousin Becky's story of how she got stuck in a glacier when backpacking in New Zealand. Stacey felt a little frightened and claustrophobic, but it turned out to be fun. The tour guide then had everyone stop at a hole in the ice. He let go of a huge chunk of ice, waited ten seconds, and then they heard it hit the bottom. He explained that the hole was roughly one hundred metres deep.

What an amazing birthday!

One day when out exploring, Stacey came across a skydiving spot. It was her dream to skydive, but she always let fear stop her. But not that day. She signed up to do it.

As the tiny aeroplane lifted off, Stacey could see the stunning views of Kaikora and wasn't scared anymore. When they reached nine thousand feet up in the air, the pilot counted down on his hand from five. Stacey knew what was about to happen. The door swung open and Rodcar, the instructor who was attached to Stacey's harness, got them into position to jump. In no time at all, they leaped out of the plane.

They flipped upside down, and Stacey could see the plane flying away as they turned back around. They were free falling. Stacey screamed, 'This is awesome!' It was the wildest feeling Stacey had ever felt.

With her savings topped back up and a loan from back home, it was time to say goodbye to New Zealand.

America was next, the eighth and final country to visit before heading back home to Wales. Stacey's first stop was Las Vegas in Nevada. Taking her first glimpse of the Bellagio Hotel, Stacey's jaw dropped to the floor. It looked like a palace.

LAS VEGAS

Stacey could see the entire Vegas Strip from the view of her room, but the best feature was the water fountain right outside of her window. The television in her bedroom played music in sync with the jets of the fountain. Stacey was engrossed. The water shot up in the air high enough to reach her room on the eighteenth floor. It was the best hotel Stacey had stayed in ever, a real treat to end her backpacking experience with.

After staying a few nights at the Bellagio, Stacey flew to visit her cousin Christopher and his wife, Clare, in Texas.

After years of daydreaming about visiting the NASA Space Center in Houston, the day finally came. Stacey saw Mission Control and mock-ups of the spacecrafts and machines that were used many years ago to go to the moon and was shown how communication was made from Mission Control up to the space shuttle and the International Space Station. It was such a magical experience.

Later that evening, Chris and Clare picked up Stacey to visit a friend. They were very excited, which made Stacey very curious.

As Chris parked the car, Stacey could see a man waiting outside his home. They walked up to the house, and Chris introduced Stacey. She stood there shaking the man's hand and asked, 'Sorry. Who is this, Chris?'

Chris replied, 'It's Astronaut Lee Morin!'

With eyes wide open in shock, Stacey thought, *I'm shaking hands with an astronaut!*

Lee began walking Stacey around his library that held over three thousand books, all of them which he had read. Stacey was in awe and couldn't take her eyes off Lee. She couldn't believe that he had been in space and had looked back at Earth.

Lee handed Stacey a bolt that had been made into a book end and explained, 'When a rocket goes into space, the bolts have explosives inside them to detach the shuttle from the rockets and fuel tank. Every astronaut who takes part in that mission gets a piece of that bolt as a memoir.'

Before leaving, Stacey asked, 'What is it like to look back at Planet Earth from space?'

Lee replied, 'If you sprinkle a little sugar on the floor, stand over it, and look down, the sugar granules are like looking at the clouds back on Earth.'

As Stacey said goodbye to Lee and got into the car with the proudest smile on her face, she thought, *Best day ever!*

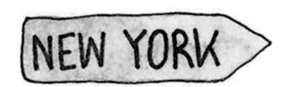

Her final destination was New York City, and her first stop was the Empire State Building. As Stacey passed floor number sixty in the elevator, her heart was beating fast with nerves. It was so high.

The views of Manhattan below took Stacey's breath away. It was out of this world.

Later that day, Stacey felt hungry so she bought a pretzel from a street stall and a delicious cupcake from Magnolia Bakery, which features in her favourite TV show. She then hopped into a yellow taxi to visit Times Square, and on her way, she got to see the Statue of Liberty, Madison Square Garden, and Ground Zero from the 9/11 terrorist attacks.

When walking through Central Park, Stacey realised it was a lot bigger and prettier than she had ever imagined. There were so many trees and a huge lake in the middle.

One morning, Stacey got up early to explore Princeton and ate pancakes at a pancake house where Michelle Obama, former first lady of the United States, used to eat breakfast whilst studying at the university. It was the perfect way to end her one-year backpacking trip.

Stacey boarded the last flight of her trip to head home, where she finally got to see her friends and family after so long. After one year of backpacking her way through eight countries, she finally completed her adventure around the world. After a year away from home it was so good to finally be back, to see her friends and family, and to sleep in her own bed.

Author's Note

Stay tuned for Stacey's next adventure book: *Stacey's European Adventures: Supporting the Cardiff Devils Ice Hockey team.*

She hopes her exploration stories have inspired readers to follow their dreams, explore, and go on lots of fun adventures. She encourages readers to write their own adventure stories below and be sure to tag her on social media.

_____

_____

_____

_____

_____

_____

_____

_____

_____

_____

_____

_____

About the Author

Stacey Suter is an adventurous and bubbly Welsh lady with a wild heart and a creative soul. She is a true explorer who is passionate about nature. If she's not writing or meditating, you'll find her barefoot in the garden while tending her plants, feeding the bumblebee's sugary water from a saucer, or out walking her local mountain with her rucksack packed with binoculars, a flask of tea, and a journal. She likes to explore with family pet Frankie the Pug for buzzards, red kites, squirrels, rabbits, or even little Mr Mouse. She lives in Caerphilly in Wales with her partner, Gerald, and her wondrous pets: Frankie the Pug and two cats, Kiwi and Kauri, who were named after her adventures in New Zealand.

Stacey is the founder of Positive Vibes & Wellbeing, which is devoted to exploring alternative holistic therapies to help others heal, and facilitates moon circles every month while guiding meditations and journaling sessions. Committed to holding space for fellow crafters, Stacey runs a local Craft & Cuppa Club and crochets blankets and other items for her Etsy shop. Stacey has featured in publications, such as *Homemaker* magazine and *Cardiff Times* magazine, and loves to collaborate with others on projects.

Instagram: @StaceySuter1
Twitter: @SuterStacey

Printed and bound by CPI Group (UK) Ltd, Croydon, CR0 4YY